Awkward Family Dinners:

A Guide to Building Better Family Businesses

Darren and Kimberley Hiebert

Praise for Awkward Family Dinners

"This is one of those books you're going to highlight so you can come back to the practical actions provided. Working with family members isn't for everyone. This book is the handbook that those of us working with family need." P. Nichols, Sounds Strategies Inc.

"The insight and personal stories interwoven are so well done." K. Powell

"I really enjoyed the book! It was an easy enough read but with practical life lessons and homework. It could also be used as a premarital handbook—learn how to fight clean!" M. Payne

Awkward Family Dinners
A Guide to Building Better Family Businesses
Copyright @ 2024—Reflek Publishing
All rights reserved.

No part of this publication may be reproduced, distributed, or transmitted in any form or by any means, including photocopying, recording, or other electronic or mechanical methods, without the prior written permission of the publisher, except in the case of brief quotations embodied in critical reviews and certain other noncommercial uses permitted by copyright law.

Disclaimer: The author makes no guarantees concerning the level of success you may experience by following the advice and strategies contained in this book, and you accept the risk that results will differ for each individual.

The purpose of this book is to educate, entertain, and inspire.

The contents of this book are not our entire experiences within our family businesses but rather moments that reflected the common and significant challenges we faced thus far. Many of the learnings and lessons have come only after going through those hard moments. These are our own interpretations and do not represent others that may have experienced things differently, unless otherwise stated.

For more information:
ISBN Paperback: 978-1-962280-21-1
ISBN Ebook: 978-1-962280-20-4

HERE'S A GIFT BEFORE YOU EVEN BEGIN!

Thank you for reading!

To help you get some additional support from the book, visit https://www.mr-mrs-ceo.com/ (or scan QR code) to access The Framework for Facilitating Awkward Conversations and our Bubble Bath Boardroom Newsletter.

To all the members of our family,
we thank you for being you,
because without that,
we wouldn't be us.
Love Always

*"Whatever else anything is,
it ought to begin by being personal."*
Kathleen Kelly (Meg Ryan), You've Got Mail

Contents

Introduction 11
It's Always Personal 11
Challenge #1: Family Dynamics 17
Chapter 1: What Are Family Dynamics? 19
Chapter 2: Who's Who in the Zoo? 25
Challenge #2: Communication & Conflict Resolution 31
Chapter 3: The Big C Word 33
Chapter 4: Competing Needs/Wants 43
Chapter 5: Clashing of Visions & Values 49
Chapter 6: Landmines 55
Chapter 7: It's Time for the Awkward Family Dinner 67
Challenge #3: Entitled vs. Earned 73
Chapter 8: Nepotism 75
Chapter 9: Them vs. Us 79
Make a Lasting Impact in Real Time 85
Challenge #4: Growth & Innovation 89
Chapter 10: Generation Gap 91
Chapter 11: Growing Pains 95

Challenge #5: Succession Planning 99

Chapter 12: The Changing of the Guard 101

Chapter 13: What's Your Destination? 107

Final Thoughts 111

Acknowledgments 117

About the Authors 119

Introduction
It's Always Personal

We've all heard the expression, "It's not personal, it's business!" For me (Kim), when I hear someone say this, I instantly think this person lacks the emotional intelligence to handle the outcome of whatever they are about to say next or whatever they have just said. It has been used against us both when a family member in our business knows what they are about to say or do will hurt us. Likewise, we both have used it in the past to distance ourselves from any responsibility of the impact on others.

What we have learned from over forty-five years in family businesses (four of them) is that it is always personal and we just hide in the business. Most people are afraid to be emotional and personal in their family business, and that's exactly why they (we) have run into trouble time and time again. If you are reading this book, it's because you have some involvement in a family business. You may be an employee or future leader of the company, but you are a stakeholder. Quite likely you are a generation pattern breaker, which is why you are reading this, to find support in building a happy(er) and healthy(er) family business that not only provides generational wealth but also a proud family legacy.

Avoiding awkward, uncomfortable conversations is not the goal of a family business. You will 100% have awkward family dinners, fierce boardroom blowouts, and strained relationships at times, no matter what. The goal of your family business should be figuring out how we can get better at managing these elements so that everyone who comes in contact with your business has the best experience possible. This includes your customers. Remember the rule: How we do one thing is how we do all the things. If you don't value the relationships within your family business, how are you showing value to those outside of it.

Let's face it, business is hard as it is, and when adding the elements of family dynamics to it, it's like being blindfolded and trying to find the light switch in a dark room—impossible! At least it can feel that way. This book aims to provide context to the reason why you might be feeling like all you do in your family business is butt heads with others. It will also provide action steps for how you can start making changes today.

The really ironic thing about family businesses is that they have a stigma of being a workplace where love and peace abound, where everyone enjoys each other so much. The real secret is that it can be a cold, callous place where no one talks of the darkness; the secrets are held by each member. No one talks about the darkness, but everyone experiences it. It's time to normalize the idea that relationships within a family business can be hard, dark, and cold, and just like any other secret, once it gets exposed, it no longer holds power. Family business is first and foremost personal.

This isn't a how-to book; in fact, we have worked really hard at ensuring it isn't because the one thing we know for sure (after having four family businesses) is that each family business has its own unique personality and personalities running them. This makes it impossible to "fix it in ten easy steps." In fact, if anyone is trying to sell you a resolution for your family business in a step-by-step format, run the other way. It's a waste of money.

This book is a navigation tool and is based on our perspective from our experience in all types of family businesses, along with interviews and conversations with many other family business owners and stakeholders. During our forty-plus years of family business experiences, we found there was very little support for people like us, like you and our families. But that's about to change! Our mission is to help identify and equip family business stakeholders with the tools, support, and resources they need to create healthy, successful businesses and families! This book, along with our podcast, *Mr. & Mrs. CEO*, are tools we use to share experiences and bring awareness and conversations to these complexities in family businesses. Through our private consulting practice, we can also provide more specific support and solutions for the unique challenges family business stakeholders face.

After all, it isn't always about increasing bottom lines, productivity, and efficiencies, it's about building legacies, relationships, and a company culture that leaves everyone it connects with feeling like they matter. The way we work as a team within the business reflects out into the way our team works with customers, community partners, and each other. How you do one thing is how you do all things! Our hope is that by sharing this with you, we can help you navigate the complexities of the relationships in order for you and those involved to have a better chance at success. After all, shouldn't your company culture be one of thriving, not just surviving?

If you are looking for someone who understands the "insider" complexities of family business, we are it. We have owned, operated, bought, and sold three family businesses and are currently building our fourth family legacy business. We have had generational family businesses to investment style "ma and pa" ones with the kids running it. We have employed our children, siblings, nieces and nephews, and best friends who felt like family, and we have found a pattern emerging among all of them. Five of them, in fact.

The five areas of challenge that we will cover in this book are Family Dynamics, Communication & Conflict Resolution,

Entitled vs. Earned, Growth & Innovation, and Succession Planning. We aim to provide feedback and ideas to help you navigate the sometimes-choppy waters of family business. The aim of anything you do should be the experience and feeling you give and get, not the numbers in your bank account. (Don't get us wrong, money matters, but not when its pursuit comes at the sacrifice of relationships.) The ultimate goal is to leave your family business with a bank account rich in relationships first, and then the wealth will follow.

But before we dive into those areas, let's look a little deeper into what a family business is and its importance in the bigger picture.

What is a family business?

When most people think of family business, it usually conjures up a picture of Ma and Pa with a son or daughter helping out the business. However, that is just not the case. Family businesses are the backbone of the economy. According to the Conway Center for Family Business, family businesses account for 64% of US gross domestic product, generate 62% of the country's employment, and account for 78% of all new job creation.

Drawing on data from Family Enterprise Canada, family-owned businesses account for 63.1% of all private sector firms in the Canadian economy and generated 48.9% of Canada's real GDP in the private sector, at $574.6 billion. They also employ 6.9

million people across the country, which is equivalent to 46.9% of private sector employment.

What does this mean?

This means that family business is a big deal, so go ahead, pat yourself on the back. You are contributing to the overall well-being of humanity, even if it might not feel like it most days.

The advantages of family businesses include a strong focus on preserving family values, traditions, and long-term sustainability. With less levels of bureaucracy, family businesses tend to be more responsive, flexible, and adaptable to the always changing economic landscapes.

And like with all good stories, there are two sides to it. The truth is, while family businesses can be advantageous and build wealth and legacy, they can also tear down, fracture, and destroy relationships in the process. As seasoned family business owners, we have experienced it all.

Challenge #1:
Family Dynamics

In every conceivable manner, the family is a link to our past, bridge to our future.

Alex Haley

Chapter 1

What Are Family Dynamics?

This is not a thesis or academic paper on the role that a family plays in the development of individuals and their impact in society but rather an overview from our own understanding, education, and lived experiences. There have been many PhDs done on this very topic, and it is not our intent to dive that deep but rather instill a curiosity into your own family and how its dynamics show up in your business.

Families serve as the cornerstone of socialization, providing individuals with essential values, norms, and cultural practices for societal integration. Within the family, individuals also acquire emotional support, love, and a profound sense of belonging, crucial for their emotional well-being. Moreover, families are the primary source of early learning, skill development, and knowledge acquisition. They are also instrumental in shaping the moral and ethical foundation that influences an individual's worldview and their interactions with the world. In summary, families fulfill multifaceted roles in molding individuals' social, emotional, cognitive, and ethical development.

This makes the family unit sound like a blissful place to be, but here's where it gets complex. The family unit is made up of individuals, all with their own personalities, interpretations, experiences, perspectives, morals, emotions, intelligence, etc., and they always collide, creating friction, conflict, and change.

I envision a family ecosystem akin to outer space, resembling a vast expanse where countless unknown particles float, colliding, breaking into smaller pieces, and being absorbed by the immense surroundings. This transformative process occurs through the unseen yet palpable energy generated by the friction when various elements are compelled together. With each passing generation, new layers of particles are introduced, their acceptance among family members remaining uncertain. This family unit, with its unique interplay of personal relationships and emotions, parallels the complexity of the business world. When the pursuit of business is introduced, with its own ecosystems and dynamics, the challenges faced by a family enterprise become notably intricate. The fusion of personal and business realms adds an additional layer of complexity to the intricate tapestry of family dynamics in the context of a business environment.

Due to this level of intricacy, when a business is introduced, these dynamics that have shaped its members are now being embedded into the business. It can create a lot of blurred lines.

It is a very complex dynamic that if you are not aware, ends up playing a significant role in your experiences within each system. One of the most impactful aspects of family roles being blurred inside the business for us has been in sibling relationships, both our own siblings and the sibling relationships of our children.

Sibling rivalry is a common phenomenon in families and can be a source of tension and conflict. While it is a normal part of growing up, the causes of sibling rivalry are complex and can be rooted in various psychological and sociological theories. A more generalized thought about sibling rivalry is that it is a competition over resources in the family, including parental care and attention.

Feelings of fairness and inequity start to cloud our perspectives of our siblings' motives. These feelings start to lay the foundation of how we view them and ourselves, and this seeps into the business relationships within siblings.

Darren's most recent insight into his very complicated relationship with his sister and now ex–business partner.

Darren is the oldest of four children (three younger sisters). His sister closest to him is younger by three years. As they became teenagers, the sibling rivalry became more intense, at least for Darren. He remembers feeling like she was always "muscling into my territory." She would try to become friends with his friends, eventually dating some of them. This led to lost friendships and awkwardness among his peers. Darren remembers being so angry with her for always wanting what he had. Sounds pretty typical for sibling stuff. However, where it starts to get complicated is when this dynamic was brought into the family business.

Darren began working with his parents at a very young age. Darren knew he would eventually take over the business; it was in his blood. However after a number of years, the business required additional office help, and his parents hired his sister. Darren remembers immediately feeling the same thing as he did when they were teens, that she was trying to "muscle into his world" again. To this day, as we embark on writing this book, he recalls the feeling as if it was yesterday . . . and as he recognizes this, he instantly knows that he has been harboring this throughout their entire business relationship. To the degree that he began to see how long he had repressed his feelings and how unfair it was to her as he harbored resentment. Not the best foundation for business partners.

With his unreconciled relationship with his sister from his teens as the foundation of a serious relationship they were entering (business partners), it is no surprise they were unable to manage many conflicts successfully throughout the years. Their own business relationship eventually became a constant source of tension, eventually leading to the permanent breakdown of the relationship and the dissolution of their partnership.

Another aspect to helping you understand family dynamics in the context of yourself is in the roles each member plays within the family unit. In the intricate tapestry of family relationships, each member assumes distinct roles that shape their interactions and influence decision-making processes. Recognizing and comprehending these familial roles can help within the business context. Having this understanding or insight can be helpful in fostering effective communication, resolving conflicts, and building a harmonious and successful working environment. Or in the very least, it will help you have a greater understanding of your own role in the interactions within your family business.

ACTION:

Take a few moments and reflect on your family dynamics.

Is there anything that pops into mind immediately? If so, write that down and see where the thoughts take you. There is no right or wrong answer when it comes to family dynamics; it's more about the recognition of them. For example, when I think of my own upbringing and the family dynamics, I would describe it as loud, chaotic, competitive, and unpredictable. So the reflection for me would be "How has this dynamic appeared in other areas of my life?"

Chapter 2
Who's Who in the Zoo?

Stop and think about the members of your family for a minute. Especially the ones who work in your family business. What adjectives would you use to describe them? For instance, who is the bossy one, the quiet one, the messy one, the clown, the strong one . . . on and on it goes. This is how we describe our family members (at times). But when you really get down to it, these labels that we so casually apply really do describe the roles each member holds, and this carries into the family business.

Identifying the role you have in your family and what the roles are for others is an interpretation of how you perceive them, but that doesn't necessarily mean that's how they perceive themselves.

For instance, my family thinks I am the bossy, strong one. Why? Because their experience as my children with me being the primary parent when they were younger told them that. I was the one telling them to get ready for school and do their homework as I was taking care of all the other household needs. Now, as adults, when they work for me, they anticipate the same behavior and see it that way; in fact they often joke around about how micromanaging I am! Whereas I think I am being clear, getting things done, and ensuring everyone's needs are met. I don't think of that as bossy but rather effective.

This also goes the other way. I am so used to telling them what needs to be done as kids, that when they began working for me, I would fall into that same pattern. It took me being aware of my own conduct and how I viewed their contributions to the business for me to step back and allow them to grow out of the role I put them in. I am not sure if they see me differently though!

One theory to get you thinking more deeply on identifying family roles is Alfred Adler's Birth Order Theory. He suggests that a child's position within the family can influence their personality and behavior based on perceived birth order roles. Firstborn children often exhibit leadership and responsibility, while secondborn children tend to be competitive and adaptable. Middle children become skilled negotiators and diplomats, striving for compromise, and youngest-born children are known for their charm and social skills, often seeking attention and exhibiting a relaxed attitude toward rules and structure.

The value of understanding more of the roles in your family is to really help you gain more insight into some of the causes of frustration experienced inside your business. Remembering that many times we are so close to the situation that it is hard to gain perspective. Leaning into doing things differently with more intention will help you have more flexibility in your thoughts. This flexibility will lead you to be open to better channels of communication, improving relationships, but also enriching the entire family business experience for yourself and others.

In our family, our oldest daughter is known as the hard worker with an intense sense of responsibility and equitability. As a child, she would tattle on anyone who did something wrong. Even if it meant her friends would get mad at her. This made her not so popular in junior high. She would care for her siblings, clean up after them, and help us with anything. If you need any furniture moved, a house cleaned, or a car fixed, call her first. She's that kind of kid. Still to this day, if there is a major problem to solve or hard work to be done, we all call her or Darren. Our second-oldest daughter, the middle child, was known as "messy Jessie" when she was a kid (sorry to call you out). She was also very social, got along with everyone, and while not lazy, she wasn't as driven with a sense of hard physical work (like me). She also avoided conflict like the plague. A typical peacemaker and people pleaser.

So when we bought a business for them to run together, their roles became evident early on. The oldest took such pride in the hard work: lifting and moving thousands of pounds of product daily, thoroughly cleaning areas of the store that her sister would not. She would be able to fix anything that broke or at least figure out what was needed. She took care of that business and had a sense of responsibility like she owned it. The other one, however, was driven more by the mission, vision, and values of the company and dove deep into learning so that she could share it all with the staff and ultimately the customers. She also took on more of the social part of running the business. She did not have a strong desire to take on the more administrative and physical responsibilities but rather the relational and communication aspects.

At the time, this seemed like a great partnership; however, because these roles they took on were more in line with their roles in our family and not necessarily what they were interested in, this too started to break down the relationship. From time to time, the oldest would get tired of doing all the heavy lifting (it was really heavy work) and then get mad and even a little resentful at her sister. This caused undue stress on the relationship. The oldest's sense of responsibility conflicted with the middle child's peacemaking, people-pleasing role.

Just reading through the definitions of birth order theory and your own sibling rivalry stories, I bet you can see who's who in your zoo. Again this is just a theory and there are a million more factors that determine and make up the psychological and personality profiles of humans, but it gives an idea of how these individuals might clash at any given moment. It may also help you, as the leader, to start seeing patterns of behavior that might be causing constant conflict, friction, and even fractures inside of the business and the family.

ACTION:

This can be done alone and doesn't need to be shared with anyone.

Take a notebook and record all the members of your family who work in your business. (It doesn't matter what position you or they hold in the business.) Now next to their names write down an adjective that describes them. This should be an honest activity; if you feel like they are the "bossy one," then write that down. Be transparent. This is how you will become a great leader. Now that you have those names/adjectives, ask yourself, "Is this true of this person? Does this person really deserve this adjective or is just how you perceive them because of your family dynamics? If you have more than one person on your list, I would start with the one you have the most challenge with. Over the next few weeks, start observing their behavior in other situations, all the while asking yourself if this person is only this way with you.

Why does this work? Because you are being more curious (flexible) and less judgmental (rigid).

Additionally, if you work with your siblings, or you have siblings working together, can you see how sibling rivalry might be affecting the quality of the relationships, or can you see any hidden resentment seeping into the workplace, perhaps tainting the workplace culture? These are great questions to become curious about.

Challenge #2:

Communication & Conflict Resolution

Because people aren't perfect and relationships are messy, we all need to learn how to resolve conflicts.

John Maxwell

Chapter 3
The Big C Word

First can we all agree that the struggle to effectively communicate is real!? Even after thirty years of marriage and many businesses, Darren and I still struggle EVERY. DAMN. DAY. (Or at least it feels that way at times!) Our very first example of this was when we were first married, just a few weeks into our wedded bliss. What you need to know is that we eloped after only a few short months of knowing each other . . . but that's another book.

We had to buy a bigger vehicle as now we had four kids between us (we are a blended family; two boys both three years old, and seven-year-old and eight-year-old girls). Darren and I discussed what kind of vehicle we were going to get, but we forgot to discuss one important part: buy or lease the vehicle. So off we went to the car dealer, knowing the vehicle we wanted. We test drove it again and said, *Yup, this is the one!* The sales guy was happy to write up our sales. So imagine his surprise when he sat down and said, "Okay, are you going to lease it or buy it," and both of us at the same time said something different. I said buy, he said lease.

When I think about it now, I feel bad for the poor sales guy as Darren and I instantly began defending our own positions, each thinking the other was wrong, and the only way we knew how to communicate our thoughts was by volume . . . and swearing (that would be me, Kim). Eventually we decided to buy the van (I think Darren still gets irritated by that!), but to this day we both still remember how poorly prepared we were to work through true oppositions of opinions to find a win-win. And we were on the same team with the same goal in mind.

In family businesses, just as in any other enterprise, the success of the business hinges significantly on the leader's capacity to communicate the vision, set clear expectations, and establish accountability in a manner that is both honest and transparent. The ability to convey this vision is the linchpin of a prosperous business, and any shortcomings in this regard can lead to discord, inefficiency, and financial strain. Within family businesses, this challenge is intensified due to the intricacies of shared history, diverse perspectives, and complex dynamics that permeate familial relationships.

Now before you close the book and go back to running your family business the "good ole-fashioned way," I want to acknowledge a few things.

First, you are running a business and have a million things at once to take care of. The last thing you may want to do is slow everything down, learn new ways to communicate, and wait for the desired outcome. Learning to communicate effectively takes time, and "slowing down to speed up" doesn't make logical sense, at least not at first, but trust in the process. You will have more time, freedom, and profits in the end.

Second, I believe that fear is the greatest obstacle for leaders within family businesses. The fear of being vulnerable. In order to develop great (or even good) communication, one must be vulnerable, and this freaks almost everyone out within a family business context. Most family business leaders are simply afraid of being seen as incompetent or weak. There is an association that if you are too kind and compassionate, you cannot run an efficient and profitable business. That you won't hold people accountable for their work, the business will fail. And that is just not true. You can be both compassionate, communicative, and run a great business. It just takes some work.

Third, if my family business was filled with conflict, unhappiness, high turnover, and high inefficiencies (which they have been), I would pick *communication* as the hill to die on. Taking the time to truly understand where and why things are going amiss will always come back to what is or is not being communicated by the leadership. The struggle is that it is not a quick fix. It takes work, dedication, and patience.

Awkward Family Dinners

And finally, if I could be so bold and honest and say that I think the communication movement inside of therapists' offices have seeped into our heads and that all communication starts with "I feel . . ." or "When you do [blank], it makes me feel . . ." This is not the communication I am talking about (although if individuals are able to learn this, overall they become better communicators, just saying).

A Crash Course in Communication

Communication can be broken down into various forms and styles, but for this purpose, let's focus on verbal and nonverbal.

Verbal communication is obviously what's spoken. It is the act of conveying information, thoughts, or ideas through spoken language. It plays a central role in human interaction, enabling people to share their thoughts, emotions, and intentions with others. Verbal communication is essential in various settings, from everyday conversations to formal presentations and negotiations, allowing individuals to express themselves, exchange information, and build relationships effectively.

Nonverbal communication (which experts say is 93% of all communication, includes various elements such as body language and tone of voice. These nonverbal cues can convey emotions, attitudes, and intentions that complement or even override the actual words being spoken. Meaning that people care more about how you say something than what you say.

Nonverbal communication is a powerful and essential aspect of human interaction, and it significantly contributes to the understanding and interpretation of messages exchanged between individuals.

Verbal and nonverbal communication are two parts that make the whole. They work together to give meaning to a conversation, context, or ideas. It also helps individuals identify if they are recognized, understood, and valued. Your family business, like ours, has a communication style from within the leadership. Whether you like it or not, how your team perceives your communication is what really matters. Not how you perceive it.

For instance, I think I am very clear and direct when I communicate. I speak clearly, check in with the listener to ensure they understand what I am trying to say, make eye contact, and ask a lot of questions to ensure I understand as well. And yet often, I get perceived as bossy. When Darren and I are trying to work together, he gets irritated with my questions and will eventually shut down. Even though I think I am communicating clearly, he is not receiving it that way. I'm not going to lie and pretend that we always work through this process in a nice and orderly manner . . . because that's not the reality. The reality is that I can become so frustrated with his defensiveness of my questions that I turn up the volume . . . and then he matches my energy, and before you know it, BOOM! A fiery boardroom blowout has occurred! It takes awareness, patience, and practice to keep the communication open and effective.

Darren, on the other hand, speaks quickly and often combines many things into one conversation and then walks away. He thinks he has articulated his needs but does not confirm that the other person has understood it. So, when something doesn't get done and he asks about it, people (me included) often reply with "I didn't know you wanted me to do that" (or something like that). This leaves Darren feeling like he can't depend on others and might as well do it himself.

Over the years, we have both worked diligently as a couple on this because we are committed to each other and want an enhanced relationship; however, that isn't often the case inside of family business. Inside a family business, people become burnt out, tune out, and ultimately give up, often referred to as silent quitting. In our opinion, the onus of responsibility for the communication temperature of your family business lies with the leadership. It is a representation of value, which in turn contributes to a positive workplace culture. When you, as the leader, take the time to understand your own communication style and the importance of it, you will inadvertently become more curious at ensuring that others understand you. When you do that, your team cannot help but start feeling more valued, seen, and heard. And when your team feels that way about your business, they will treat your business the same way! Simon Sinek says, "Customers will never love a company until an employee loves it first."

The Cost of Miscommunication

It doesn't take a rocket scientist to know that miscommunication is the undoing of any great relationship: employee, family, or both. It can also be the takedown of a business. Over many years and many family businesses, we have been victim to this ourselves, with the end result being the breakdown of relationships and unexpected outcomes. We have talked to many other family business owners who have been cut off or cast out of familial relationships because of poor communication in the business. Darren and I have our own story of being cut out of a crucial relationship leading to an early business exit.

Darren's sister (and business partner) became a very good friend of mine. Over the course of twenty-five years, we enjoyed all the things that friendships offer, including traveling together with our spouses, family dinners, and sharing holidays. The relationship was made stronger between us because our families overlapped in business. It was also why, when our friendship experienced some deep conflicts, it impacted others in the family and business, specifically Darren's partnership with her.

Darren and her had been in the family business together for many years, and like many family members running business together, they had their own fair share of business conflicts that over time started to wear down the relationship. All of this came to a head during an extremely vulnerable time for me and Darren. I had been diagnosed with breast cancer at the same time he was experiencing burnout (after forty-five years of working) and increasing frustration with key partners in the business.

It was during this time that she and I started to experience some deep conflicts that required both of us to work together to find a resolution. She refused to do so and has not spoken to me since.

The abrupt change to the relationship created a lot of curiosity within the family and the business, but no one really dared to ask about it. Meanwhile, Darren was going to work every day and running a business with her. This became an elephant in the room that they both ignored. I know Darren did not want to acknowledge the fall out between me and her (as it was not his business) and having awkward conversations is not his strong suit. His inclination is to ignore things. I cannot speak about her thoughts, but she made no attempt either; they both chose to not communicate about a deeply personal event and how it may impact their business relationship.

What ended up becoming so obvious to Darren was that he was not aligned with his key partner's values. In fact, in doing this book, he shared that he knew they didn't share the same values right from the start but he didn't think that was important back then. He just put his head down and worked. This realization was the final straw for Darren. He wanted out, and immediately. It became the catalyst to his exit. He has barely spoken to his sister since that time. To this day, this fractured relationship between all three of us is felt deeply within the family and the family business. The loss of this crucial relationship between me and her, and him and her, comes down to communication, or lack thereof. It has impacted the reputation of a family legacy that once was held with respect and proudness, to one now clouded with broken relationships and hurt.

Signs that your business may be impacted by poor or lack of clear communication include a high turnover of staff, struggling to get results or meet goals, a continued sense of frustration for yourself or others, or a loss of significant relationships inside the family business.

ACTION:

Draw a line on a piece of paper (down the middle), and on one side write down a few key words that you use to describe your communication style. Title that side "How I communicate."

On the other side, write down key words of how you think your team perceives your communication style. If you don't really know how they perceive you, try asking around and see what they say.

Does how you think how you communicate match with how your team perceives it?

Chapter 4
Competing Needs/Wants

Communication is often assumed. People think that they have communicated clearly, but the reality is many times assumptions are made. People tend not to check and see if they have been understood, if the other person has "picked up what they are laying down." Within a family business, this is way more complex. There are so many assumptions made of the members of the family and the business, and these assumptions become the foundation for how you react, communicate, and essentially build your business. And while there are many factors at play, one core element is competing needs/wants.

Needs are such a basic core essential of human beings: need for security, safety, love, belonging, connection, etc. Needs for individuals are always driving behaviors, actions, and perceptions, whether you are consciously aware of it or not. Hint: Most times we are not consciously aware.

One interesting aspect to humans is our nervous system and our flight, fight, or freeze, response to threats. Long story short, way back in the day, if you felt threatened by an animal or something that would take your life or resources, your body would go into an automatic stress response process. This response still goes on today, except now the threat is related to resources that allow us to feel secure/safe (e.g., housing, food, healthcare, love, etc.). We as humans have needs, and they are all different, so what might threaten your sense of security/safety might not threaten mine. But here is what happens when this stress response has been triggered: our brains cannot strategize, think clearly, or make good decisions as *all* of the body resources have been called into preparing us to physically fight or flee. Your actual ability to problem-solve and think clearly through a complex situation is at its lowest at this time. These types of triggers of our nervous system will cause us to lash out, react, push back (fight) and in some cases, walk out (flight) or shut down and not respond to anything (freeze) before anything is resolved.

Becoming more self-aware as to what and when you are reacting versus responding is a great place to start observing your own behavior. Remember this isn't a quick fix, it is a process that takes time to evolve, and there is no perfect response. It is about reducing conflict and learning to communicate. We recently had the following situation that quickly got away from me where my daughter's need for growth clashed with my need for freedom. Her actions were threatening my sense of security. My actions were threatening her need for security (making more money), and the clash was messy!

Chapter 4 Competing Needs/Wants

Our daughter had been running one of our businesses for about seven years, and we relied on her heavily. When we started the business, it was never our intent to work it. We were the investors. It was a ten-year commitment, and seven years into the commitment, things changed. She wanted to move on to something more challenging. After all isn't that what most of us want in our professions? To grow more competent, experience more challenging opportunities, and expand our impact, income, and confidence? All things every parent would support their children with.

Well in this case, I said I wanted that for her, but internally I was conflicted (but I did not acknowledge that). While I wanted growth and expansion for her and to see her fulfilled, it meant that I would no longer be able to have the freedom I wanted. It meant I would have to postpone some of my goals. At the same time, she was struggling with her own people-pleasing tendencies. You see, she's the oldest in the family, the one who takes care of everyone else, who prides herself on "taking one for the team," and she knew this was going to upset us. She didn't want to disappoint us, especially me. Needless to say, her exit was messy.

Both of our own personal needs got in the way for either of us to handle the situation in a way that respected each other's needs and goals. For months after, I would describe it as "when she left us," creating drama around that statement. Reinforcing to her that she in fact did let us down and reinforcing in my own mind that she was the problem. Not my greatest moment as a parent or a boss.

It was so uncomfortable for her that when she did start work with another organization and was struggling, she refused to reach out to us. As the oldest, who was now mad at her parents, she was determined to show us that she didn't need us and that she could make it on her own. The real heartbreak here is that she needed our support during that time, but this business conflict tainted her ability to reach out and our ability to be available. We felt she needed some space (again an assumption we made without clarifying). We thought we were respecting her right to separate from us and to include us in the conversations when she felt she wanted to, so we didn't reach out much. Months later when we started to unpack this conflict and to reconnect, she told us she felt she didn't matter to us anymore now that she wasn't working for us. Again, you can see how all parties made assumptions about the others' needs and what really ended up happening was more distance in our relationship. For a further breakdown of this conversation, you can check out our podcast *Mr. & Mrs. CEO* episode 13, "A Daughter's Voice."

Like any major upheaval, if you are able to be self-aware, allow yourself the time you need to remove the initial reactions and bring some calmness to yourself; you will be better equipped to work through the situations while maintaining relationships.

Chapter 4 Competing Needs/Wants

The difficulty is in identifying all the needs and wants of all the players. The business needs/wants, family needs/wants, and the individuals needs/wants. These things collide often; however, when people collide over the big things, it can be catastrophic to the relationship and the business.

Darren has worked in a family business his entire life. Literally the only job he has had. Started with his father, then his mother. Years later, his sister joined, a nephew, and throughout the years nieces, nephews, cousins, and our sons and sons-in-law. To say he's had his fair share of arguments with family members over business is an understatement. I think he is the master of awkward family dinners!

However one day he came home and declared to me with such certainty that he was *done*! All the fighting, frustrations, and conflict was no longer worth it to him. He was going to sell off his shares and leave the business. Now, this wasn't the first time he threatened to sell, but this time it felt different. I freaked out on the inside. I instantly started trying to calm him down and convince him that he was just tired, or overreacting. Basically ignoring what his needs were at the time. I thought I was helping him.

After all, why would you want to walk away from a successful business? Didn't make sense to me. The reason why it didn't make sense to me was because my core need for security was threatened, and it scared me to my core. My need for security was clouding my ability to be present for my husband while he was going through his own struggles. I had to take a few moments to step back, recognize where my perspective was coming from, acknowledge that I was worried about the financial implications, and communicate with him when he was calmer. This allowed us to come up with a plan that met both of our needs.

ACTION:

The difficult part of the needs/wants is to really learn and become more aware of *your* needs/wants and when they are motivating the behavior. Here are some questions you may ask yourself to get some insights.

- What makes you feel secure?
- Where is your risk tolerance?
- Is it the same as others in your family business?
- Have you talked to other family members about these kinds of things?
- Think about a time that you overreacted to something someone wanted to do that would impact you. Can you look back on it and identify what feelings that brought up in you?

Chapter 5
Clashing of Visions & Values

In the dynamic landscape of any business, the role of values and visions has become increasingly pivotal, shaping the very essence of organizational identity and direction. Values serve as the moral compass guiding decision-making, while visions act as an aspirational roadmap for the desired future state. Together, these elements form the bedrock upon which businesses build their reputation and navigate the complexities of the marketplace.

The alignment of values and visions defines a company's character, influencing strategic decisions, employee engagement, and long-term sustainability. This alignment establishes a framework for success and resilience in the face of challenges. This need is no different within a family business where the complexities demand a centered and grounded organization with up-to-date vision and values.

The challenge arises as attention and resources dedicated to vision and values within family businesses are often lacking.

Assumptions are made that familial ties automatically align with the business vision.

For us and our varied family business experiences, especially as younger business owners with no formal training in business, the concept of vision was vague and oftentimes confused with goals and dreams while the term *value* was something that we thought mattered to us.

The other thing to lean into here is that vision and values change. These are not static statements that are done once and live on forever. As the individual changes over time, as the leadership rolls over, and as the economic landscape and societal values change, so do your vision and values.

Most times inside of family enterprises, you will have a value that was established by the founder, then passed on by action (others watching) to the next generation until one day, someone challenges it. Most times challenges to family business vision and value are extremely personal. It can feel like a rejection. Imagine rejecting a family value that a man's worth and value are determined by how hard he works physically.

In Darren's generational business, the value that was passed down was work first. This was how men took care of their families. This was how men became "men." You sacrificed time with your family to provide food, shelter and whatever else. It didn't matter how tired, hungry or lonely you were. It's what you do as "the man." This was also societal values at the time (when his father was young). When Darren became the leader of the business, guess what his value was? Yep, the exact same. So when anyone opposed that value by refusing to work overtime or by wanting time off to go to the doctor, they were met with pushback. Now as the generations have changed in his business, this has become more of an issue—the clash between old values and new ones. It got to the point where one of our children who worked there realized he had different values than that of the family and that caused him quite a bit of stress. Eventually he left that family business to find employment that aligned with his values. One day not long ago he said, "Imagine being the one guy in the family that rejected the values of a generational family business."

The point is as family members, leaders, and stakeholders inside the business grow and change, maintaining harmony between individuality and collective identity becomes challenging. Differing perspectives, life stages, and personal aspirations can lead to conflicts, requiring open communication and a commitment to finding common ground.

That's what a vision does. It keeps everyone moving in the same direction. Imagine being in a canoe and you as the leader didn't share where you were going. How would the other members support you? Some would paddle one way, some the other way. Yes, they would all be paddling (doing something), but all their paddling was getting you nowhere.

Ultimately, the challenges lie in managing the dynamic interplay between individual growth and collective values in the family unit and business, requiring continuous effort, communication, and a shared commitment to sustaining the essence of the shared vision.

When Darren and his sister became partners in the family business, it was assumed that they held the same vision for the business. As first-time business owners, they only knew what they experienced and what was modeled before them from their parents. He took care of the labor force, sales, innovation, and she took care of all the administrative/financial tasks. Looked like a perfect match. They had both been functioning in these roles for years before, and the business was doing well so it appeared they both had the same vision and values for the business.

Unfortunately, as Darren changed over the years, it became clearer to him that he no longer shared the same vision and values. For years he ignored it as there was a lot at stake: all the family members involved, the financial impact, his own level of comfort dealing with confrontation. Eventually he could not handle the misalignment as he felt the friction all the time and knew he wasn't being the best business partner. He decided to speed up the succession plan and leave the business a few years before planned.

Vision and value statements are additional forms of vital communication between your business and its operators (all of them). With any communication form, practice makes progress (never going for perfect), and progress makes way for attainment.

ACTION:

Vision Check: Go around to your organization and ask every member what the vision is of the company. There are no right or wrong answers. Let them tell you how they see it. If it's helpful, send them all an individual email so that they can reply in writing. Review responses. Are they seeing what you see for the business? Are there some different answers?

If you are a partner, when was the last time you and your partner(s) reviewed your business visions? Perhaps it's time to gather the troops and get refocused. A boat with all paddles rowing together gets further faster and with less energy used.

Value Check: Values are often written down and displayed on the company's wall, lunchroom, or office, but remember values are caught—meaning values are determined by actions not words. What values does your business profess to hold? Are your actions as a company reflective of what you say you value? Your business might say it values "family" but yet you expect your workforce to work an exceptional amount of overtime. You might hold an annual family picnic to support your family values, but in reality your day-to-day operations suggest otherwise. As a leader within your organization, it is important for you to spend some time analyzing this. Some indicators of incongruence of your written values with the values of your actions include high turnover rates, confusion of roles, an inability to make decisions within the organization, etc.

This is also a task that could benefit from you bringing in an outside resource to support your family business in developing and redefining on a yearly basis.

Chapter 6
Landmines

Conflict happens. Just like shit happens, so does conflict. And in family business, it is guaranteed to happen. In fact, the conflict inside of family businesses is usually fueled by unresolved conflicts related to other things as well as the business. The family relationships are so complex as they live in a variety of experiences, not just the business. Your interactions with family members within the context of your family will set the stage for how you will all interact in the business. These are the added layers that only family businesses face when it comes to conflict and conflict resolution. And how we manage these serious disagreements over and over again will dictate what type of landmines are waiting to blow!

Let's start by defining conflict as it relates to this topic. Merriam-Webster Dictionary defines it as "to be different, opposed, or contradictory, to fail to be in agreement or accord."

In order to understand how to resolve conflict, you first need to know how you handle it. Since the object of this book is keep things really easy to process and relatable, I am including the five styles identified by Kenneth Thomas in 1971 (and since refined by him and his colleague Ralf Kilmann). These are widely used, particularly in discussion of management styles. It is also a great team activity to have everyone go through and identify their own conflict style. It can add a layer of understanding for the teams and leaders. Below is the list.

Turtle Behavior (Avoiding)

When acting as a turtle, people tend to hide in their shells to avoid conflict and confrontation. This avoidance might be more important to them than their goal or the relationship. Sometimes, when people are being a turtle, they will give up on their goal or end a relationship rather than face up to the conflict or issue. It can involve a decision that, at this time, it is better to avoid conflict than to confront it.

Shark Behavior (Competing or Confronting)

When acting as a shark, people are more concerned with their goal than the relationships. If they must choose, they will often choose their goal at the cost of the relationship. Being a shark often involves using authority or power-over, ignoring or intimidating others, or using threats or violence.

Teddy Bear Behavior (Accommodating)

When acting as a teddy bear, people value the relationship more than their goal. If they must choose, they will often give up their goals to help maintain their relationships or to support other people. Sometimes people acting as teddy bears believe that sticking up for their goals in a conflict will damage a relationship, so they let the other person have their way. Sometimes, they are willing to set aside their goals because they believe the value to the relationship is greater than the benefits of achieving their goals.

Fox Behavior (Compromising)

When acting as a fox, people are moderately concerned about both their goals and relationships. In seeking a compromise, they are willing to give up some of their goals in return for the other person giving up some of their goals. They seek a middle ground where both sides gain something.

Owl Behavior (Collaborating)

When acting as an owl, people value both their goals and their relationship: they respect their own goals and care about the other person's goals. As an owl, conflicts are seen as a problem that can be solved (rather than a competition) and as having the potential to strengthen relationships. The aim is approaching conflict in ways that helps build the relationship and discover ways forward that satisfy everybody involved. This is often called a win-win approach.

Did you see yourself in any of these?

Darren is like Jekyll and Hyde; he has two different styles. At home he is a turtle and a teddy bear. He's the easiest to get along with and is most always willing to compromise. However, as a business leader, he is a shark in disguise. He becomes passive aggressive when someone presents as a block to what he wants. He will fight a bit for what he wants, then he will walk away as if he's over it and then go do whatever it is he wanted to do. This caused many fights between him and his father and eventually him and his future partners. One time, Darren asked his father if they could build a specialized product to sell to a customer; his father said, "Absolutely not." Darren walked away and did it anyway. His father caught him that night working away at the special product even after telling him not to. Now, when Darren looks back at how he managed this type of conflict, he sees things differently. Back then, all he saw was someone standing in his way; he could not understand how his dad might feel or what his father may have wanted.

As for me, I am an owl. Not always though. Through education and a career in social work, I have come to learn the value and importance of collaboration. In doing so, I have become comfortable with addressing awkward conversations and moving people toward resolution. The thing about being an owl is not everyone is comfortable with it. I can often be mistaken for being "direct." As business partners, Darren and I can often struggle with effective communication as he can be passive aggressive (still) and I want to talk everything through to a win-win.

So now that we have given a basic framework for understanding how different people may handle conflict, including yourself, let's look at the power of unresolved conflict and how to recognize it. The purpose here is to help you develop a framework of sorts to start unpacking how to manage the fiery boardroom blowups.

Darren and I still on occasion have a fiery boardroom blowup. We have the added commitment of our marriage to help us prioritize healthy conflict and resolving conflict in a timely manner whether it's business or personal. We have recently begun to call a timeout if one of us is feeling like we can't manage the conflict reasonably. When we were much younger, neither of us would be patient enough, and it would either be a fiery boardroom blowup or the silent treatment. Neither of those have good outcomes. Conflict resolution takes time and patience; two things humans are always running up against!

Perhaps one the biggest fuelers to managing conflict effectively is unresolved conflict. This applies within any context, be it personal relationships or professional settings. Unresolved conflict shares a striking resemblance to landmines lurking beneath the surface. Much like these concealed explosive devices, they have the potential to detonate unexpectedly, causing widespread damage and upheaval. Think about a time when you and a friend, partner, or family member had a small argument and suddenly *boom*, it erupted, catching you off guard, and before you knew it, you were bringing up things from long ago and saying/doing things that were extremely hurtful, uncalled for, and most times irreparable.

Let's face it, within most family structures there is a great chance that there is some unresolved conflict lurking underneath the surface between its members. It's quite common for family members to sweep things under the rug for the sake of the "family." However when these same people then enter the business arena, these old, unresolved conflicts don't just disappear. They are like landmines; they pose a constant threat to the integrity of the relationships and the business.

I remember when we were getting ready to open one of our businesses with our daughters. They were young moms at the time, each with their own struggles. They were very close in age and spent a lot of time together. Needless to say, they had had their fair share of disputes along the way. However, as we were preparing to open this business, one of the daughters was giving off angry vibes while the other was not. There was some tension in the air for sure. I decided to try and address it so we could all get on the same page for planning, and unbeknownst to me, it was a landmine. I asked what was going on, and it was like lighting a match in a room full of gasoline vapors . . . Boom! Suddenly they were yelling and screaming at each other about things that had nothing to do with the business and everything to do with past hurts and unresolved conflicts. Keep in mind, they are sisters and they have a long, shared history.

Here is the point I am trying to make. As family members, you have a long, shared history that will likely have some unresolved conflict hidden within, and now add business, which will bring its own matters of conflicts. Now you have two very potent igniters for an explosive event. And while most people don't like conflict and try to avoid it as much as possible, it's this avoidance that is the actual culprit to unresolved conflict. Managing conflict effectively will be one way to ensure you are not adding additional unresolved matters to the landmines.

There are a number of ways in which you can set yourself and your team up for success in healthy conflict resolution. Gary Chapman, the author of *Everybody Wins*, states, "As surely as you can learn to ride a bicycle, drive a car, or use a computer, you can learn how to resolve conflict." Like most things, it takes time, energy, vulnerability and a willingness to go first. Those also happen to qualities of great leadership. You grow first, the others will rise.

As for me and Darren, we continue to grow our skills and comfort levels in the area of conflict management. We look at it as another skill (just like any other skill) that requires practice. Acknowledging and allowing room for ourselves and our team to manage conflict openly and without ramifications is a core value and one we strive to maintain. There is no perfect balance; it's a practice that needs developing not mastering.

TIP: Managing Awkward Conversations

I call conflict management "awkward conversations," and over the course of a fifteen-year career in social work and managing hundreds of awkward and volatile conversations, alongside operating multiple family businesses over thirty years, I have become comfortable with it. I have developed a framework that I use every time I know I have to address an area of potential conflict. This framework is not about perfection, it's about taking the time to set everyone up for as much success as possible by eliminating some contributors to conflict escalation. Below is the framework I try to use every time or, if I didn't use it when I am reflecting on a poorly managed conflict, I use this framework to see what elements were missed. Recognize that as a business leader, and especially of a family business, managing conflict and having awkward conversations will happen, possibly daily. It's your role to set the tone, creating the culture you desire by your actions, not your demands.

Context: You are meeting one-on-one with a family member that is a partner or team member in your business to discuss performance issues, an error or behavior.

Environment Check: Is the environment clear of distractions, interruptions, and other employees that are not involved. Is the room a comfortable temperature and a place to sit comfortably for the duration of the meeting? Phones and other electronic devices should not be present unless there's an agreed-upon use for them.

Time: Ensure you set the meeting at a time that is good for all parties involved. Create enough of a time buffer for unexpected conversations and for others to process the information you are delivering. Do not "squeeze" it in between other meetings that have no flexibility.

Prepare: Take some time to write about your feedback and then re-read it and remove phrases like "you always," "you never," "you aren't," and "you did it again." Challenge yourself to provide feedback without all the personal blame, just based on the facts. If possible, ask an HR expert or mentor to review the feedback you have written up. Be open to learning.

Conversation: I start the conversation by stating the obvious (remember we are all people trying our best, and in this case we are likely family members). I start out by acknowledging that this may be an uncomfortable and awkward conversation for both of us, but it is something that we must work through. If it is their first time dealing with you as a leader in the business (as opposed to being a parent, sibling, or other family member), it may be hard for them to separate you from the family, which can make it a little more difficult for them. Again, as the leader, you are setting the pace and tone for the culture of your business; you go first, others will follow.

Suggested Script: "So, I want to talk to you about a few things that keep happening during your shift, and it might be a little awkward or uncomfortable for us as we are family, but it's super important for your growth and that of the company."

Identifying and normalizing the feeling of awkwardness or uncomfortableness lets everyone relax a bit. For me, it lets my team members know that we are both experiencing the same thing. The key point is feeling the *same*. It reduces some of the perceived or real power imbalance.

Next, bring up your topic. Be direct and clear. Say as little as possible. In my experience, talking too much as a leader will eventually get you in trouble. There is power in fewer words. Allow the person to receive the information (by staying quiet) and then respond to it. Let them explain their understanding of the events. Ask questions that are curious in nature, not judgmental. Key questions to ask to get more information are to ask, "And then what?" or "Can you tell me more about that?"

The biggest takeaway here is to get as much information as you can to understand where and how the subject matter occurred so that you both know what and how to avoid it in the future. Most times if patterns are repeated, it's because parties are misunderstanding each other in some way. You want them to feel heard and understood just as you want them to hear and understand you. Conflict management is not a one-way conversation.

If there are a lot of emotions (crying, etc.) and they need some time, give it to them. You can ask them, "Do you need some time to process this information?" I also allow them to cry it out there—just take the time to allow the emotions. It is my experience that typically people don't want the uncomfortable to drag on. Also, recognize that people feel bad when they let someone down or need to be corrected. Your job as a leader is to show them it is safe in your business to learn and grow responsibly.

To end the conversation, make sure to summarize how you are moving forward. What interventions, strategies, or tasks will be done and by whom? Clarify that everyone understands.

Let them be upset or mad at you (respectfully, of course). People need time to sort through their emotions; make sure to set a follow-up meeting to revisit the matter so both you and the team member have clarity moving forward.

And my final piece of advice: Sometimes people do not respond as maturely or cooperative as you wish, and some conflict outcomes may be out of your control. We cannot control how others respond; what's most important is that you reflect on your management of it and review for your growth.

ACTION:

Which type of animal best describes your conflict style?

Identify which one best resonates with your style. Does your style change depending on what's at stake? More importantly, how does this play out in your business and what can you do to improve?

What about the other members of your family business? Can you identify their conflict resolution style?

Do you hold any unresolved conflict with other family members in your business? Be brutally honest with yourself. Are you open to developing a plan of action on how to resolve it? You may need outside support with this. Don't underestimate the power of taking the time to sort this out.

Chapter 7
It's Time for the Awkward Family Dinner

As owners and operators of four family businesses, one of the top questions we get asked is "What are your family dinners like?" and our response is always, "We are experts in awkward family dinners!"

Truth is, our family and extended family dinners are no different from yours. I bet there are topics of conversations at your family dinners that can cause an instant blowup, am I right? Or there are family members that you don't particularly like and try to avoid like the plague, making the family dinner awkward. In our world, we just have more topics that can cause fights and more people who paste a smile on their face and say how lovely you look, all the while stabbing you in the back in the workplace. Sorry if that went dark for a moment.

I (Kim) was not used to a family that grew a business together. I was used to a family who yelled, swore, and even physically fought each other over random things like clothes, friends, and cigarettes, and when we didn't want to be a part of the family, we wouldn't. When we were ready to be a part of the family again, we would apologize and then be back in the family, no harm no foul.

So when I married Darren and entered his family, it was an eye-opener. For instance, he would come home from work *furious* with his father after having a big argument and threatening to quit, and then later that same evening we would all be having dinner together, acting normal even though he and his father did not talk things out. I thought it was weird, but I soon found out this was his normal.

As we grew our own family and other extended family members grew theirs, there were more people involved in the various businesses, so managing home and work relationships got more complex. The arguments over business matters seeped into many crevices on all levels of the family. Gossip, hearsay, and the opinions of many would float around taking on its own identity, like the old game of Operator. (If you don't know that reference, Google it!) However, at times the tension would become too much, and *boom*, an eruption would occur.

Over the years we have tried to instill "rules of engagement" for our family dinners, but they still get broken. You can often find two or more people in the corner "talking shop." Just like in other families, members share their own work-related matters.

Chapter 7 It's Time for the Awkward Family Dinner

However, when you have the majority of the family working in one or two of the same places, it can make the dinner table feel like a boardroom. So we do try and table the shop talk so things aren't so boring and we can enjoy other aspects of each other. It also helps define our family time.

I am not sure what's more awkward though, sweeping things under the rug or managing the conflict head-on. Personally, I find sweeping the big things under the rug and smiling and pretending everything is fine very hard to do. Darren is a master at it. And this last year, we were both put to the test.

This past year was perhaps one of the hardest times for us as it relates to family and business. The situation impacted multiple generations and many members of the family and hit us pretty hard. It was a very public and personal attack on Darren and me, made in the name of business. The attack was launched by a very close family member who was also being supported by other close family members. This person attempted to absolve themselves of any personal impact by claiming, "its business, not personal." It was devastating to us and our own smaller family structure. It was deeply personal.

Let us share that for us, this time and the actions that were taken were extremely hurtful, shocking, and unexpected. This was an extended family member of Darren's, who Darren regarded with respect, pride ,and admiration, making this experience by far one of the hardest times in his life. Our kids were concerned about their father; I was concerned about him.

People inside of separate family units were divided. Siblings, parents, spouses, even our grandchildren were involved. Before we knew it, it seemed like an "us versus them" mentality had hit our own small family unit, and more fractures occurred. Things were getting really intense, and Christmas was looming.

And while the attack had some financial impacts and threats, the most expensive part of it all is the broken relationships . . . the broken trust . . . the betrayal. These take time to work through, and it wasn't just Darren and me that it impacted. So while we (and other family members) were nursing some deep hurts, we were now having to figure out how to come to terms with having some of them in our home, celebrating with us as part of our family. Do we all smile and tiptoe around on a landmine field the entire time, or do we detonate the landmines that we know are active and ready to blow?

So, as someone who isn't afraid to detonate landmines in a controlled environment, for me it was a no-brainer. Let's get a third-party mediator involved to mediate our own family tension! I started to pose this as an option to our family. The majority of them were not really in favor of it but would do it if I insisted. Darren did not like the idea at all, but he too was at a loss for how to manage the family holidays.

Chapter 7 It's Time for the Awkward Family Dinner

I sought out advice from the matriarch of Darren's family, his mother. As she was very aware of the situation and had been in some of her own similar ones over the years, she has maintained great relationships with the people that are important to her in her family, even her great grandchildren. Here's the advice she gave us.

Not everyone wants to work things out and just because you want to doesn't mean everyone has to do what you want; you can't make them. So you are the one that has to figure out how you want to act.

Straightforward, direct, and truthful. Gosh, I love the wisdom age brings!

This wasn't a new concept for either of us, but it landed differently this time. It was the reminder that it was okay to let the hurt and betrayal we were feeling be absorbed by forgiveness and grace. It released us of the anger and bitterness that was building. We were then able to host our own holiday celebration with grace and love, and no awkwardness—at least on our end.

Challenge #3:
Entitled vs. Earned

Nepotism is something that happens in every field.

Soni Razdan

Chapter 8

Nepotism

"Nepotism—the practice among those with power or influence of favoring relatives, friends, or associates, especially by giving them jobs."

Oxford Language Dictionary

We are 100% guilty of nepotism. I often say that we make our kids pay us back for their tuition, braces, weddings, and sports by working for us as adults. All of our children have worked in our four businesses at any given time. Qualified or not.

Our oldest daughter moved away when she became an adult. Far enough that we couldn't see her daily, weekly, or even monthly. So when she had her first child, we all flew down to see her, her partner, and her baby for a week. When we left, it was horrible. We all cried. She was building her life in the new place, her partner's hometown, but she wanted to be home, and we wanted nothing more than to have her home. So, Darren offered him a job in the family business. He had no experience at all. We wanted our daughter and grandbaby close to us, and this was her wish as well. Darren used his family business as a way to offer employment and a career for the young man, even though he wasn't qualified.

Nepotism has its perks, but it also comes with a reputation for "entitlement" or an impression that relatives don't actually earn their way in the business.

One of our other businesses was staffed and managed by non-family members. Right from the start, the manager would tell me that if any of my kids came to work there, she expected the same things from them as she did everyone else. She would go on about not being a babysitter and cleaning up after the owner's kids because the kids are entitled. She hadn't even met my kids at that point. I did bring one of my daughters into the store to be trained, and the entire time they were met with an unwelcoming hostility.

Having family and non-family employees can breed tension in the workplace. Non-family members can feel threatened for myriad reasons, either perceived or real. In the story above, the employee was feeling threatened but also felt confident enough to tell me her expectations for my kids working there. She perceived them as entitled without ever meeting them or observing their work habits. Her own fears and past experiences colored the way she looked at all family employees.

Darren's generational family business has had the most experience with hiring family members as it had the biggest operations. Although employees were made up of family and non-family members, leadership positions were only held by family members.

The reality is any family member who "gets" a job given to them is typically getting an opportunity to show that they can learn and grow into the business, add value, and be a team player. They basically are skipping to the "front of line," forgoing the application and interview process.

On the flip side, we gave a daughter the opportunity to build and run a million-dollar business with no experience. It was on-the-job training. In our eyes it was a great opportunity for her; in her eyes it was not a "real job." She often talks about when she wanted to find a "real job" after working in our business for seven years. She did not recognize her accomplishments as hers. She was thankful for the opportunity and the skills she learned, and now as she works for a non-family business, she is getting feedback about herself from the outside world, which has given her confidence and pride in herself in a way she wasn't getting from us, and that has been beautiful to watch flourish in her.

I was chatting with a friend who told a story about when she was in her early twenties and went to work at her father's business. She remembers thinking there was no way she would get fired because she was the boss's daughter. Her father, in all his wisdom, made sure he was not her direct supervisor (his company was big enough to have other managers/leaders), so she was placed under another partner's supervision. She shared with me how she wouldn't do any work and when her supervisor would hold her to task, she would just be sassy and sluff him off. Eventually he fired her. Again, the opportunity was presented, and it was hers to win or lose; in this case, she lost it.

ACTION:

Think about the last family member you hired. Did they go through the same interview process as a non-family member? What did you skip over that you would not have if they weren't family? How could you adjust your process so that a more equitable process is in place to support anyone who applies?

How do you or your organization manage family member employees?

Chapter 9
Them vs. Us

Another dynamic at play inside of the family business is the separation of family and non-family employees, or a "them versus us" culture that can be easily created. Symptoms of this are lowered productivity, high turnover of staff, or poor morale among the team. These indicate that your team is not quite as aligned as you might think. Your non-family employees see the behaviors of everyone very differently than you. They have a level of personal attachment removed and are better able to actually see the values, culture, and conflict resolution at play in the business. Remember communication is mostly nonverbal; it's not what you say but your actions and tones that tell the real story.

Oftentimes when non-family employees don't work out (they quit or we let them go), it becomes a "we just can't find the right person" problem. After over forty years, in various forms of family businesses, as leaders, employees, and stakeholders, we have had our fair share of turnover, and we can tell you that it is more often a leadership and culture problem than a "them" problem. You may say that everyone is treated the same, paid the same, but the activity in your organization is speaking a different language. Inequity or a feeling of unfairness will often silently and quickly divide the members of an organization.

The other factor at play that you as a family business leader are working against is that when push comes to shove and the hard decisions have to be made involving job security, the non-family employee will be let go first. Case in point: COVID. During the pandemic, both of our businesses (like so many others) were impacted. For the smaller business, I had to reduce hours of the staff and even let a few go. Two remained. My daughter and her team lead. I then had to let one more person go as our revenue had dropped so significantly. Guess who I let go? That's right, the team lead, not my daughter. Both of these employees were hard workers and great at their jobs, but at the end of the day when push came to shove, I chose to maintain my daughter's employment over a non-family member. I felt terrible but would have felt more terrible if it was my kid. I had a bias.

The same thing happened with Darren and his business. During COVID, they had to lay off everyone at first, except of course, the immediate family members. Eventually things came back around and everyone was brought back, but the message was clear. When it comes down to it, family employees have more security than non-family employees.

Same thing when mistakes are made or there are performance issues. Often there is a perception that relatives have more leeway for mistakes or that their poor performance issues are not met with any real action or consequences.

Many years ago, a relative was working in the family business. He was new to the industry and inexperienced in the dynamics of a family business. He had a charming but somewhat cheeky demeanor. There are stories of him confidently asserting to other employees that he would never face termination because he was related to the boss and that the business would eventually be his. Despite his youthful ambition and cheekiness, he began to display a lapse in professionalism that became a growing concern. This became problematic for the other leaders in the business, but the individual in question was hesitant to address the issue adequately. He had personal reasons for this reluctance, including a strained relationship with the family member and a desire to avoid conflict within the family. The individual's lack of diligence escalated to the point of causing harm to another employee and company property, turning his behavior destructive and aggressive.

This situation created significant tension among other business partners, fostering the perception that family members could evade accountability while non-family employees were consistently held responsible. This not only harmed the financial aspects of the business but also affected its overall culture. Ultimately, the family member had to be let go. It was a challenging decision for the leader, knowing it would strain the relationship, but it was necessary to safeguard the well-being of the company, its people, and its partners.

Leadership positions and promotions within a family business is also another area of bias that contributes to a "them versus us" culture. Everyone, and I mean almost all humans, want to evolve and grow in their craft. They eventually tire of doing the same job and want to be challenged with a position with more skill, more responsibility, and be able to contribute to decision-making, creative strategy, and other functions of the business. This is no different in family business. But where it does differ greatly is that very few family businesses (exceptions would be the large/mega businesses) plan or prepare for this evolution of their labor force and leadership team. The positions of leadership are typically held for the family members, whether they are qualified or not. We (as the decision-makers) almost always award family members higher-ranking positions before they are ready for it, regardless if there is a better-equipped non-family member. Darren looks back over the forty years in his business, and guess what, the only positions of influence and leadership in his family business were held by family members. Any non-family member that was given the opportunities in these various roles never succeeded.

Being a family member employee can influence your interactions with non-family colleagues. It can be challenging to be perceived as solely the boss's kid or the owner's sibling, carrying a subtle suggestion of not entirely earning your place. This dynamic adds complexity to the workplace environment. Non-family employees often value the concept of "earning your stripes," and despite the family member's hard work, there may linger a subtle question of whether their position is truly earned or perceived as entitlement.

ACTION:

The best thing to do is start assessing your company's behaviors, specifically around the performance review process, or the write-up process that is used consistently. This is how you as a leader will start to create a more equitable culture.

Does your company have a rubric or metrics to assess performance along with pay structures and promotion opportunities?

Do all employees have access to training opportunities, regardless of how they are related?

How does your company award promotions, raises, or leadership opportunities? Is there a clear process for this?

You may even want to consider bringing in an HR consultant to help assess and build the necessary procedures that clearly define the processes.

Make a Lasting Impact in Real Time

"I alone cannot change the world, but I can cast a stone across the waters to create many ripples."

Mother Teresa

There is one question that I've asked hundreds of people:

If you knew what you were called to do in this life, what would you do?

Most people either don't know what their true calling is or they're afraid to take action in ways that are deeply meaningful to them.

Would you do something that takes one minute if you knew it would help someone live to their true potential? Achieve their goals? Build lasting relationships, both personally and in business? Change their relationship with money? Be a better leader? And most importantly, stop judging themselves by other people's values and learn to feel exhilarated about life and its possibilities? If so, I have a favor to ask you.

There are people all over the world who dream of living a life where they truly feel fulfilled. They know they are meant for something more but don't yet know what steps to take to find inner inspiration and live true to their own highest values. This book can help them. But I need to be able to reach them first.

Here's where you can help.

If you've found this book valuable so far, would you please take sixty seconds right now to leave an honest review wherever you bought the book? This costs sixty seconds of your time and could be the reason someone chooses to finally change their life.

All you have to do is say yes and you will join a movement that will help others:

- Understand that family business is personal
- Be the pattern interrupter in their family business
- Dare to do things differently
- Understand the complexities of family business
- Find harmony and success while building a family business
- See the benefits of having a people-first strategy

We can create a ripple effect that will change the world, one person at a time.

If you decide to leave a review right now, thank you. You are part of the movement. In the rest of the book, you will discover even more ways to discover your own infinite potential as a leader within your family enterprise, and by sharing this message, you also help others do the same.

Just remember, a ripple effect can reach farther than you ever imagined.

Thank you for helping us. I appreciate you!

Challenge #4:
Growth & Innovation

Strength and growth come only through continuous effort and struggle.

Napoleon Hill

Chapter 10
Generation Gap

One of the more serious pain points inside a family business is a generation gap. As younger stakeholders (but not yet decision-makers), the ideas for growth, innovation, and scaling are like weapons of mass destruction for the leaders, especially if the decision-makers are your parents. The clash of "generational gap" is not new; in fact it is always at play, but inside of a family business it can be like a brick wall.

Darren began working with his father at the age of seventeen. At that point, his father still looked at him as his son first, which means "father knows best" and didn't consider his son qualified enough to add any value about business growth. This perspective comes from the fact that as a father, he has watched, taught, and participated in Darren's growth from infant to adult. His father has lived experience of when Darren didn't make the best choices or was witness to young Darren's reckless driving antics. (Darren loved cars so much, it is why he left school and started working for his father.) These experiences shape the relationships, and it becomes hard to see people differently. The same goes for young Darren. As a kid, he couldn't see the value of his father's wisdom; in fact most times kids think their parents' rigidity is the reason they aren't getting what they want.

This is a very common relationship dynamic. Think of your own parent–child dynamics. We (as parents) have had more experience and know that kids still have a lot of learning to do, no matter the age. After all, we as parents have taught our children to become competent, contributing members of society, and it is in the teaching that has informed how we view them: always as learners, never as experts.

This for me (Kim) became evident when we started a brand-new business that my daughters were going to run. It was their first time as leaders and businesswomen, and that meant they didn't know anything (in my opinion). The first few months were fine, as we were all learning, but eventually it became clear to them that I was micromanaging them. And to be honest, I was. Especially about sharing information. The girls would laugh and say, "You better ask what she wants you to say, we can't say anything without her permission." You might be thinking, "Why were you like that?" Well, because as teenagers and young adults, I struggled with some of their decision-making, and that came through when it came time to trust them with our business assets (not the money, the reputation). I was the block and not open to see what they could bring to the business. Hindsight is always 20/20, and Darren and I both see how we both became the blocks to the next generation of business.

In order for any business to thrive and stay relevant, it needs to be able to grow, scale, and expand. In business language, that means innovation, technology, and scaling. You simply can't do what you've always done . . . you will eventually become extinct. This is especially true with artificial intelligence showing up on scene. Things in business will be done quicker and more efficiently, and in many cases even create the demise of certain industries. Scary and exciting all at the same time.

This presents a challenge for all businesses but is especially true for family businesses. When you have parents that are the boss/leader and you are trying to bring new ideas to them, if they don't see you as you see yourself, then it'll trigger your parent–child conflicts of the past. We have seen this time and time again. It's the battle to be recognized and validated. The amount of times Darren and his father would fight over Darren wanting to bring in new technology or new services and add to the business is countless.

For years and years, Darren would come home from work madder than a bull claiming, "I *quit*! He won't listen to *anything* I say!" Or he would walk off a job and have his father chase after him. You name it, they fought over it. It was a true clashing of the minds. Darren is a young and reckless kid in his father's eyes, while Darren sees his father as the old, rigid guard, unwilling to listen to the value and innovation he wanted to bring into business. For years this went on.

However, one day it was Darren who was the brick wall with anything new in the business. His younger nephew is now in the challenger spot. Coming in with new ideas, concepts, and technology that Darren didn't understand and didn't care to; after all, he was successful doing what he was doing. His rule of thumb became similar to his fathers: "if it ain't broke, don't fix it." It was during this time that Darren began to really feel what it was like in his father's shoes and instantly found himself having more respect for him.

ACTION:

As the leader, do you feel you are always in some kind of tug-of-war with younger generations' ideas for your business?

If so, consider opening up the dialogue and replacing the word *no* and *but* with *yes and*. Using "Yes and I will think about that," or "Yes and how does that align with our company vision?" or "Yes and how will that support objectives?" allows for the opportunity to be curious and explore with your team. Try it out and see how it opens up a dialogue instead of building walls.

Chapter 11
Growing Pains

Family businesses, while often characterized by strong bonds and a shared history, can face significant challenges when it comes to achieving sustainable growth. One major hurdle is the reluctance to bring in external expertise. In many family enterprises, decision-making is quite often confined within the family circle, which can limit exposure to fresh ideas and innovative strategies. The resistance to seeking professional advice or hiring non-family members in key roles may impede the company's ability to adapt to evolving market trends and capitalize on new opportunities. This insular approach can hinder the business from reaching its full growth potential.

Moreover, family dynamics can sometimes blur professional boundaries, affecting communication and decision-making processes. Personal relationships within the family may impact the objective evaluation of business strategies and hinder the implementation of necessary changes for growth. Tensions arising from disagreements in both familial and professional spheres can create an environment where critical decisions are delayed or compromised. Navigating these interpersonal dynamics while striving for expansion requires a delicate balance that not all family businesses successfully achieve.

Case in point. A number of years into business ownership, Darren found himself always in conflict with the operational ideas of his younger partner (who was also a close relative). He thought to himself, am I being the "brick wall," shutting down the innovation and growth that my younger partner sees? So in an attempt to not be the brick wall, he conceded all operational decisions that fiscal year. The outcome that year was far below normal expectations, proving to Darren that he knew better how to run the business.

However the problem wasn't about who knew more about the business, the trouble was the two of them did not effectively work together recognizing and respecting the roles and wisdom they each brought to the table to develop a successful growth strategy for the business. They didn't consult outside supports or even develop an actual strategy that would support the operations. Managing growing pains, like many other things in a business, takes time, intention, and communication. Inside of a family enterprise, these things can all be made more complicated by familial relationships.

Generational gaps, family dynamics and economic stress are all factors that impact the growth and sustainability of your organization. The older leaders like to stick with the old way of doing business, especially if they have experienced considerable success already, making it harder for the younger, less-experienced relative to make an impact. One of the ways to tackle this is to really look at how the business is functioning as a whole: what are the pain points it's experiencing and what are the possible solutions. Innovation is the mother of necessity. The action section below has some starting points you may find helpful in determining areas in need of innovation.

ACTION:

Below are some of the more common pain points for businesses that suggest some innovation or growth strategy is required. Use this with the other stakeholders in your family business as a way to get them involved with developing strategies. You are the leader, not the one who knows everything.

New Hires—Do you have a high employee turnover? Or perhaps you require more labor but you don't have the manpower for thorough onboarding and training? Perhaps it's time to consider using some resources to develop a standardized onboarding and training program. What technology is available to help this? Is there an outside person who can be contracted to support this?

Redundancies—Are there things in the business that are repeated by the same people? Can it be collapsed or integrated into one process? Create a list of them and task someone to capture them, record them, and research how to reduce them.

Inefficiencies—These can be things like mistakes, call backs, unpreparedness—this can all lead back to a lack of standard operational procedures (SOPs), lack of proper standardized training, or difficulty identifying key performance indicators (KPIs) for your organization. Ensure the entire team is aware of them.

Challenge #5:

Succession Planning

30% of family businesses survive the transition from first to second generation ownership. 12% survive the transition from second to third generation. Only 13 percent of family businesses remain in the family over 60 years. And 47% of family business owners expecting to retire in five years DO NOT have a successor.

SCORE.ORG

Chapter 12
The Changing of the Guard

"When will he just sell me the business? When will he give me what I deserve?"

These were some of Darren's thoughts as a young son building a business with his father. Darren wanted the business badly. He did finally get the business (with his partner), but how it happened is not what he or anyone expected.

The family business was abruptly interrupted one day when a phone call delivered the news that his mother had suffered an aneurysm, leaving her in a coma. This unexpected turn of events had his father stepping away from the business to care for her. With their absence, Darren and his sibling continued with the responsibility of running the business. However, the constant uncertainty surrounding their parents' involvement created a stressful atmosphere that hindered the progression of the business. The lack of open discussions and succession planning between Darren, his sibling, and their parents exacerbated the strain on their relationship. The parents did eventually agree to the sale of the business to him and his sister, but it was definitely under duress.

Darren took the reluctance of his parents wanting to sell them the business as his dad not wanting him to be more successful than them and it wasn't until years into his own reign that he understood the reluctance. The reluctance had nothing to do with Darren's ability, it had to do with his father not wanting to let go. The business was the last thing between him and his mortality. It represented his entire life's work, his sacrifice for his family, his contribution to the world. His father also knew how deeply the family business destroyed relationships, changed people, made them greedy for power and money. Darren never got a chance to ask his father more about this, as sadly he passed in 2006.

As second-generation owners, Darren and his partner did talk about succession planning. They had identified a successor but hadn't really put the plan or timeline together. Then an unexpected event occurred, creating a need for that plan to be formalized. As leaders, they had already been discussing the idea of succession planning, so when it was time for Darren to leave, it was an easier process. Darren wasn't selling under duress. He was ready to leave, and the successor was eager to take over the robust business.

When Darren looks back at his younger self making demands of his father, he thinks, "What an entitled, spoiled brat I was." Age and experience really do bring about a wisdom that youth cannot fully appreciate until they find themselves in the same situation.

Succession planning, or an exit strategy, should be a part of the beginning discussions. Without out, it leaves the business, its assets, and the families it supports vulnerable. Vulnerable to insecurity, loss of income, and loss of legacy. It also creates additional stressors on familial relationships. We only have experience in small business, but think of the billion-dollar family empires and greed and desire to take over! It's stuff that movies are made of!! The series *Succession* comes to mind.

So if succession planning is so vital for any organization, why is it so difficult to do for family business?

In our experience, there are two main reasons why this has been difficult, and they both center around hard conversations. Within family enterprises, it always comes back to communication and relationships.

First, there are few people who like to talk about the end of anything. Think about it, starting your business out by talking about how things will end is kind of a bummer, depending on where you are in life. It's kind of like talking about a prenup prior to getting married. Thinking about ending your reign as a business owner will undoubtedly bring up issues of your own mortality, and that in and of itself brings up big feelings, thoughts, and anxieties. Talking about your ending in something you are deeply committed to is a challenging conversation. I think in some ways it goes against our human nature to think of endings or death. It requires time to process along with a high degree of emotional intelligence.

Typically, many founders, leaders, and stakeholders of family businesses do not have the confidence or skill set to manage these complex discussions within the family business ecosystem because many family units have an unwritten code: we don't talk about hard things. And in the day-to-day stresses and demands of businesses, it's easy to push aside these awkwardly hard conversations about the future that no one really wants to talk about.

Second, succession planning requires finding the person or people that will take over. In family businesses, this can be extremely difficult. With each new generation comes changes to the entire economic environment. How many families take over the farming business anymore? Values, ideations, and employment options change with each generation. The modern-day family business owners, regardless of industry, must make the discussions and planning of succession early on, inviting others into it, exploring different possibilities for the future growth of the business outside your own self.

ACTION:

Set some time aside, think about the succession plan, and answer these questions:

1. Is there a clear plan for the future?
2. If so, can you articulate it?
3. Is it still the same?
4. Are all the people involved aware of it?

Consider holding a meeting with the stakeholders and start the discussion of the future plans. Refer to the framework for awkward conversations available in this book.

Chapter 13
What's Your Destination?

Have you gone on a trip with no destination in mind, no idea how you would know if you arrived, or when to know when to leave and move on to the next destination? While that may seem idyllic and have a place during a long, adventurous sabbatical, it is not a strategy for business, and yet for many businesses—in particular for family business—this is exactly the strategy in place.

Many family businesses are "founder" businesses. By this, I mean the family member is the founder of the business, the one who bootstrapped it, nurtured it, took care of it, and grew it. The one who believed in it when others didn't. The one who went all in and went without for the sake of business. Sounds like parenting to me! Jokes aside, parenting and founders have a lot in common.

For instance, when you bring a child into your home you don't start planning for the end of their lives with you. No, you start with the basics: feeding, sleeping, diapering, connecting. Your focus is on getting to know the needs and growth. When you first start a business or even take over one, typically you do the same, focusing on getting to know the business, its needs, and its growth from there. And like parents, the end seems very far away, a distant matter to deal with when the time comes.

For us, some of our other more independent businesses didn't really have succession plans, they were more our exit plans. It wasn't really about who would take them over but rather when we would sell them. But that too requires more thought and planning than one might realize. Selling a business is not an overnight process. It can take years to find the right fit, similar to succession planning. That's why it's something that should be part of the entire business plan from the beginning.

Our most recent sale of a business of ours was a *disaster*! We had started thinking about selling it at about the five-year mark (out of ten). We knew from previous experiences that selling businesses was not a fast process. So we started the process, albeit very passively. Two years later, a pandemic, economic changes, and ever-evolving staffing problems made it very clear we needed to sell, and quickly.

After being toyed around with tire kickers and window shoppers, we decided to be very aggressive in our pricing and vetting process. When we finally found our buyer, we were in such a rush to release it that we overlooked some details that left money on the table and the transition to new ownership messy. Not our best business performance in dollars or in aptitude.

The reality is without planning ahead and being extremely intentional and purposed, we leave succession planning/exit plans to circumstances and crisis, neither of which are recipes for success in business. It can make exiting out of a business tumultuous, stressful, and risky. When things are left up to force or circumstances, leaders and stakeholders make poorer decisions; they aren't able to be objective of the needs and how best to support the individuals or the business.

Remember that succession planning/exiting isn't just about you, it's about how you set up others for success. Your legacy should include the ending, not just the beginning of an empire.

ACTION:

1. The unwritten code ("we don't talk about hard things") is actually prevalent throughout family businesses and causes myriad other issues affecting the daily operations and success of the business. Look around your family business leaders. What are you *not* talking about? Can you identify the unwritten code in your family business?
2. Are you currently an employee of a family business and want to own it or a portion of it one day? Does the current leader or owner know your desires? Perhaps

you aren't qualified yet, what do you need to do to make that happen? Write out a list? Do you need to take a course in business, get more experience, talk to the stakeholders? Whatever the steps are to reach the end (which is really the beginning of the next phase), you should write them all down and start making your plan.

3. If you are currently an owner or stakeholder in some kind of a family business, what is your end goal? How will you know when you are getting ready for exit? Is it an age, or maybe a revenue goal, or maybe it's an operational goal? If you haven't thought intentionally about it, why don't you? Is it a hard subject to engage on? These are signs that you need some support moving through the emotional parts of the process.

4. Write these things down, have a shareholder/leadership meeting, and discuss these things. Find out what the other stakeholders' thoughts are on succession planning or their exit.

5. And finally, if you are the person in charge, consider hiring an outside source to bring your leadership team through this process. It is much easier to have someone else facilitate these complex conversations. It will also allow you to add your thoughts without objection.

Final Thoughts

We love the unity, community, and shared experiences that come with family businesses. We love to share our learnings and at the same time learn from others in the family. We are always trying to improve how our team members (family and non-family) feel and experience value under our leadership. Like everyone else, this is a process not a destination for us. There is no perfect, only progress.

We chose these five challenge areas because after many years of family business experiences from almost all the different levels and structures, we found that these five are the most prevalent and yet the least talked about, and the last thing that family organizations invest in. The people.

Talking about the challenges (or in this case reading about them) is our way of saying "we see you" to all of those involved in family enterprises regardless of your role.

The challenge areas presented in this book are not just specific to family business as many organizations have similar challenges.

The thing about family business is that the management of these challenges demand for its leaders and stakeholders to be skilled in people strategy. Many of the smaller family business leaders have become leaders by working their way through the business. Typically, resources are used for driving revenue in the business, and often, investing in people strategy and development of leaders is least important, or in many cases, never even considered.

Think about it, as a business owner, you will send your staff to take courses on skills that will make them better at their actual job in order to make your company more profitable—the ROI, if you will. It's an easy exchange when you can see more physical money coming into the business. You might even enroll yourself in some courses to learn different aspects of business (accounting, inventory management, marketing) to enhance the bottom line. It's an easy justification.

What's harder to assess is the ROI of enhanced relationships, a more cohesive labor force (everyone rowing in the same direction), and a happier workplace. Yes, most leaders say it's important to them, but let me remind you, *action* defines what's important to you and your organization, not words.

If your family business continues to have interpersonal conflict, it has become known in the family as a source of continued stress and friction, or you are exasperated with the underperforming and ongoing staff turnover inside the workplace, your organization needs to start focusing on a developing a people strategy not just the revenue-generating skills. Equipping your staff and team with conflict management, communication, active listening, and personal advocacy skills are just some of the ways you can start to take action in this area.

We are currently working on our fourth (and *final*) business, which also is a family business. We continue to use our past experiences as teachable moments for how to navigate current ones. We seek outside counsel for matters that require objectivity that we cannot hold. We are patient in the five challenge areas, understanding that every action we take impacts our relationships with our family, our team, and our clients. After all, collectively they are very personal interactions that make up our business.

Now don't get us wrong, this is not an easy task. Developing and implementing a people strategy is not a common practice in smaller businesses, and especially in family businesses. I have seen large companies and government agencies do it; in fact it becomes part of the development process and is mandatory for promotions. I realize they are large organizations and have the infrastructure to allow for a more developed process, along with the budget, but that is where innovation and resourcefulness comes in. Finding a way to develop your people strategy for your unique business might very well be a trailblazing activity. And like any trailblazer, there is work to be done. It's not always easy, and it's never fully appreciated by those who currently surround you. In fact they may present some challenges, but those who follow you get to walk that path you blazed. And that, is how legacies are built!

Family first, transactions second.

When You Still Want to Burn It All Down, Here's What to Do Next!

There's no limit to your potential!

Reading this book is the beginning of your journey, and it's an important first step.

Here's how we can help you continue to explore the use of your newfound clarity, sense of purpose, and inspiration to build a better family business.

1. Access all your free bonuses.
   By reading this book, you've unlocked every bonus and resource my team put together to help you maximize your success.
   Visit www.mr-mrs-ceo.com to get everything for free.

2. Join our Bubble Bath Boardroom Newsletter.
3. Hire us to speak by emailing hello@mr-mrs-ceo.com.
4. We share invaluable tips and resources to help you move further along your journey. Let's connect on our social platforms and reach your success together!

https://www.instagram.com/darren.hiebert/

https://www.instagram.com/kimberley.hiebert/

Acknowledgments

To Darren's parents who are the original trailblazers. Without their hard work, love, and commitment, we wouldn't be where we are today. They followed their faith, believed in the possibility of an expanded future, and never gave up. We thank you for all you've given and role-modeled for us, this is where your legacy began.

To our kids and grandkids, you are the reason we continue to grow, expand, and find new heights. You are our legacy. (PS And also a big thanks for letting us share some of your stories, you'll get extra in your inheritance . . . if we haven't spent it all . . . hehe).

And a great big round of gratitude for our friends and family who encourage our ambitious adventures, support us during all the hard times, and celebrate the victories with us! YOU GUYS ARE OUR ROCK!

And finally, a special mention to Jake Kelfer and his team at Big Idea to Bestseller for keeping us focused and excited to see this project come to life!

About the Authors

Celebrating three decades of marriage, Darren and Kimberley Hiebert are the dynamic duo whose journey through the highs and lows of life has shaped them into resilient entrepreneurs, proud parents, and passionate advocates for the complexities of family businesses. Their family story is as rich as it is diverse—a blended family with four kids, eight grandkids, and two furry companions.

Kim's background, marked by adversity, saw her rise from a high school dropout and foster kid to a successful social worker for over fifteen years. In 1990 she took a leap into entrepreneurship, expanding a popcorn company that skyrocketed to a million dollars in sales within its second year. She then added two specialty retail businesses, with the help of the kids, and Darren of course. Kim's successful journey through entrepreneurship exemplifies that success doesn't require a predetermined pedigree.

Darren, influenced by his entrepreneurial father, entered the business world at age twelve, spending summers working in the family business. A high school dropout at grade eleven, he hustled to buy the company in 2005, evolving over forty-five years from a dedicated worker to a business owner and eventually seller of the generational business.

In 2023, Kim and Darren launched the *Mr. and Mrs. CEO* podcast, a raw and honest exploration of the complexities they faced throughout the years of family business. Recognizing the scarcity of resources addressing the challenges of family business, they embarked on sharing their experiences. This led to the creation of their book, a heartfelt compilation of anecdotes, insights, and action steps to support others. Through their work, they aim to shed light on the less glamorous aspects of family businesses, emphasizing that others are not alone in facing dark days and sunny days alike.

By sharing real-life examples and providing practical exercises, Kim and Darren hope to guide fellow stakeholders and leaders through the intricate journey of family business, offering clarity on why things happen the way they do. Their message is clear—success in family business may be challenging, but it's a journey worth taking together.

Made in the USA
Columbia, SC
22 May 2024